As They Knew Her

Shawna Nicole

As They Knew Her

By **Shawna Nicole**

As They Knew Her By Shawna Nicole

© 2020 by Shawna Nicole Published by Afangideh Publishing

P.O. Box210394

Montgomery, Alabama

Photo Credit: Dreamers Photography by Adrienne Quick

ISBN: 978-1-7331480-7-8

Acknowledgments and Credits

Cover Design, Cover Photo, Editing & Integration, and Back Photo: The Dynamic Adrienne Quick of Dreamers Photography in Prattville, AL. Girl, you did your thang, as you always do! I am forever grateful!

Thanks to each one of those people who helped pray this book into completion! I would list them ALL by name, but I am bound to forget a name. The first ones who come to mind are Rodney Brannon, Pastor & Lady J Ellison, Penny Genous, Lorraine Petty, Jennifer Priest, and Tasha Scott, to name just a few.

Please know that I am forever thankful to all those not listed for your love, support, encouragement, and prayers! Every bit of it was received!

A very special shout out to "My Boo", Rodney Brannon for letting me bounce ideas off him and for giving me constructive criticism while asking the hard questions. You rock!

Dedication

I dedicate this book to the loving memory of my mother, Barbara L. Wright Pointer, who is gone but certainly not forgotten.

I also dedicate it to those who can identify with the content within, whether personally or someone you know closely.

This book is for you.

The labor that has gone into getting these pages published is in hopes that they can help someone along the way to a place of healing, forgiveness, reconciliation, and celebration.

~Shawna Nicole

Foreword

Our calling is how we impact people while we are living but our legacy is how we impact them when we are gone.

Shawna has found a way to embrace her calling while honoring her mother's legacy.

This book will serve as a mirror for any individual who desires understanding, peace, and reconciliation in their lives and through their family. When Shawna first approached me about writing this book, I was excited for her.

It is important to tell our stories. The process of birthing our stories to share with others is a transformational process for the purpose of helping and healing others while we, too, are being helped and healed from the inside out.

In this book, you may find yourself thinking of your own life and the people in it.

Shawna does a beautiful job of showing us her journey of healing and wholeness while encouraging others to do the same. It is a beautiful journey.

Tasha M Scott

Professional Speaker | Leadership Trainer | Life & Executive Coach | Inspirational Author

Maximized Growth, LLC

Contents

Introduction

T his book paints a picture with details about some of the life events of Barbara Lavern Wright Pointer from the stories of family members.

While the book shares personal information, there are more truths about her life that were not revealed.

I must rely on hearsay for some of the details, since many of the events happened either before I was born or when I was very young. This book expresses my view on the events and how it affected me.

It is my intention to be forthcoming; to show you the good and the bad while praying you walk away with some divine truth about how life's circumstances can lead you to many different paths.

If you read this book and you find your life peeking out from the pages, rest assured this does not have to be the way your life ends. There is a Savior who willingly gave His life and died on the cross for your sins and shortcomings (and mine). You can live a redeemed life so that you may above all things be in good health and prosper mentally, physically, and spiritually, even as your soul prospers (3 John 1:2). The rest of your life can be the best of your life!

If you walk away with hope restored or courage to face your giants, then my writing will not be in vain. I have tucked the details of this book away for many years because of fear and shame. I feared rejection from others because of some details of my mother's life.

Now, I stand unashamed because scripture tells me I need not be ashamed. Here I am, both naked and unashamed in Christ, the hope of Glory. My silence has served no one well. I have come to understand that secrecy helps the devil. It is where he dwells.

I no longer feel the need to apologize for my inadequacies, because everyone deals with times of feeling inadequate about something.
We all have secret struggles, whether big or small. If you tell me that you do not, I will not believe you.

The Garden

Shawna Nicole, 1994

I am one of God's roses

He planted me in a particular season

at a particular time, for a particular reason.

He is pruning me daily with much love and care. Constantly

refining my beauty for all to share.

Sometimes I sway in the wind, but he does not get mad. Instead,

He keeps me from falling and for this I am glad.

God helps me to grow by shining his sunlight down. He waters

me with precision in a fertilized ground.

He strengthens me when thorns are removed.

Allowing me to be approachable as barriers become reproved.

He teaches me wisdom; God is my sword and shield.

I have learned to depend on him and to do his blessed will.

Bugs and insects desire to destroy me, but God says, "Not so."

No weapon formed shall prosper by stranger, friend, or foe.

I will rejoice in the things that God has made. I am thankful for

the blessings in life he gave.

AS A DAUGHTER

This excerpt of stories focuses on the colorful tapestry made from the perspective of a mother who knew her daughter. Barbara's mother had many vivid memories of her. These are but a few.

She was born on October 21, 1957 to Helen and Leon Wright. She was the firstborn daughter, and people both near and far looked on and admired her beauty. She was a sweet child; well-mannered and intelligent, just like her dad. She was a beautiful baby with dark skin, big brown eyes, pigeon toes and bowed legs. I would walk down the street with her, and people would just stop us and give her money.

~Helen G.

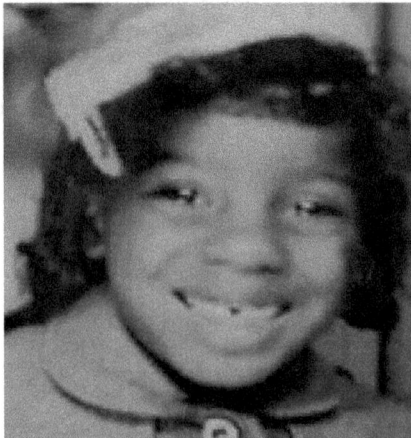

(picture of Barbara Lavern Wright)

THE GRAPEVINE

N o, this is not about the song, "I heard it through the grapevine" that many have come to know and love from the late 1960s. Oddly enough, the event I am referring to happened when Barbara was about 9 or 10 years old, making the song relevant and present for this era of time. The story goes that Barbara went out in the alley that had grapevines overhead, ripe for the picking. She and her brothers would go out and stand under the grapevinewrapped lattice to pick grapes.

The only problem was that there were swarms of bees present as well to do their job. As my mom was taking her time gathering the plump, juicy grapes, a bee flew up the back of her dress! She began to scream and holler loudly! I am sure it must have felt like the pain would never end.

Her younger brother, Johnny was there and tried to come to her rescue. He stuck his hand down the back of her dress, trying to scoop the bee out and away from her. The harder he tried, the more the bee stung, and the louder Barbara got! Their dad John W., the only dad my mom knew, rushed downstairs when he heard all the screaming. He asked what was wrong and when he found out, he acted quickly without a second thought.

He ripped Barbara's dress straight down off her back and the bee stopped stinging, after what must have felt like an eternity! He got some tobacco, wet it, and rubbed it on the sting, taking the pain away.

When I heard this story, I could picture my mom frantically moving around trying to rid herself of the bee. This story is a great example of some of our lives. We may have found ourselves in this same predicament. I do not mean getting stung by a bee, though that may be the case as well. I am referring to you crying out in despair because you were hurting. In that moment, your heavenly Father was right there with you and stepped in, "Johnny on the spot," (pun intended) during your despair and your painful experience. He was present in your trouble because He never leaves you nor forsakes you. You have endured some painful experiences in your life but God has helped you through each and every one of them. He was right there, putting a healing salve on the areas of your life where it was needed.

Maybe there are some areas you felt entitled to hold on to the pain and refused to allow healing to take place. Perhaps, you wanted people to understand your frustration, or you may have viewed it as a badge of honor to grip it. If that is your story and you want to release that extra load you have been carrying; I invite you to pray this prayer.

PRAYER

Lord, it hurts so much to hold on to this stinging pain but the thought of releasing it makes me feel even more defeated. I ask that you rip off each layer of thoughts that would keep me trapped and hurting.

Right now, I am going to choose to be free and walk in wholeness. I am not sure exactly how to do it because I feel like I have been gripped by the pain for so long, but I know that you will guide me into the truth. I am trusting in your word in I Peter 5:7 that you care for me, so I am casting every concern that I have on you, knowing that you are well able to bear each burden. The long-lasting pain was meant to cause me harm but you removed the stinger!

Thank you for allowing me to walk in new victory! AMEN

Psalm 55:22 (AMP)

Cast your burden on the LORD [release it] and He will sustain and uphold you; He will never allow the righteous to be shaken (slip, fall, fail).

COOKING

B arbara liked to cook, and sometimes, when she came home from school, the chicken would already be seasoned and waiting. She would fry it up hot and fresh for dinner. Some of her favorite foods to cook were fried fish and cornbread, oxtails, and fresh neckbones. I would put the neckbones on the stove and turn them down low.

When Barbara came home, she would finish cooking the neckbones and add vegetables to the pot when it was time. She would eat the neckbones with such passion and so intently that I would say, "Don't hurt yourself, Barbara!"

Those neckbones must have been mighty good to her. I love to cook and to bake as well. The thing I have learned about cooking is that you must follow instructions. Whether they are written out or given verbally, there is a method to preparing food that makes it taste good. If you have cooked certain items many times, you know what to put in the pot to season it or how to mix the batter so that the cake comes out moist and delicious. That takes practice and attention to the details of the recipe.

Just like cooking using recipes, the bible contains our recipes and instructions for success. Using the bible will be key to having good outcomes and flavorful living. It will take practice and application.

Psalm 34:8 (MSG)

Open your mouth and taste, open your eyes, and see—how good GOD is. Blessed are you who run to him.

PRAYER

Thank you, God, for times of reflection from those who knew her and loved my mom. Thank you for the similarities I share with my mom. Help me to use the recipes and instructions for success found in the bible. You are so sovereign to provide us with an all-inclusive recipe book. AMEN

ON FIGHTING

"She tore the clothes off the boy. He was a big boy.
She was always getting into fights, but she fought mostly guys," her mother
said. "She was strong and she would win."

I have often wondered about the force that propelled my momthe fury behind her fight. Is it normal for girls to have the desire to fight guys and win? I do not think it is. Did anything happen to warrant these forceful feelings and emotions? I can only imagine the inward struggle that went on inside of her.

There is always a motive behind violence. Either a person has been cheated on, abused, bullied, and teased, disrespected, or neglected. There is a "good" cause, a justifiable cause (at least in their mind), as to why they feel the need to lash out and retaliate. While I have never fought a guy in a fist fight, it is not because I did not want to. I even had dreams about it and had good motive and reason. I think I resisted the urge because I felt too small and helpless. Maybe I did not have the right amount of rage.

There was an incident when I was younger that made me very angry, to the point that I made a rash judgment. This event really taught me how out of control I was, and I decided to repent so I would not continue life with that degree of anger fueling me. I understood how anger could lure you into very poor choices and causes you to think and behave irrationally. Anger is not a sin, but it can lead you to a life full of regrets if you allow it to overtake you.

Ephesians 6:10-12 (MSG) And that about wraps it up. God is strong, and he wants you strong. So, take everything the Master has set out for you, well-made weapons of the best materials. And put them to use so you will be able to stand up to everything the Devil throws your way. This is no afternoon athletic contest that we will walk away from and forget about in a couple of hours. This is for keeps, a life-or-death fight to the finish against the Devil and all his angels.

With that truth in mind, we must fight! But when we do, make sure you are fighting the right way. Do not fight against your family, children, spouse, friends, or even enemies. When you fight, recognize the real adversary, and use the word of God in fervent prayer and you will always be victorious!

PRAYER

Lord, thank you for providing all the weapons we need to fight with! Thank you for the privilege to pray the word of God in your name and for giving us testimonies of victory against our defeated foe. We praise you for showing us how to fight and win. Thank you for the revelation that we lose when we fight flesh and blood!

In Jesus' name. AMEN

LONG WALK HOME

My grandmother told me that one time, in the wee hours of the morning, the doorbell rang. It was my mom. She was bloody, beaten up, and half-dressed in the dead of winter, a cold winter with at least 6 inches of snow on the ground. My mom would sometimes just leave, and no one would see her for days at a time. This time, she said she walked back to Newark from New York.

Someone had beaten her up and kicked her out of the car. She was hungry, cold, battered, and bruised.

It is a sheer miracle that my mom made it back to New Jersey in one piece, so to speak. She endured all this and bore, in secret, the specific details of the event. She certainly was not in one piece emotionally and mentally.

My mom had to be strong to live through such trying times in her life. Perhaps this is the reason she turned to alcohol and drugs. She needed something to mask all the pain she was in emotionally, physically, and spiritually.

I do not know everything my mom had experienced up to this point, but I can just imagine how she felt as she took that long walk back to New Jersey.

During our lives, it may be worth confessing that we have felt times of being beat up, outdone, and broken. Just as my grandmother took my mom in to tend to her wounds, it is so encouraging to know that God is inviting us to come home so he can mend the broken places in our lives. He can put you back together better than you thought possible because He is the creator and has specific plans for your life.

Jeremiah 29:11

For I know the plans that I think towards you, thoughts to prosper you and not to harm you. To give you an expected end.

PRAYER

Lord, for those who need to take a sobering walk back home, may you allow them to complete the journey so they can begin the mending and healing process. Let them know that you are with them in every step. Allow them to feel your loving arms wrapped around them as you engulf them with your presence.

In Jesus' name. AMEN

I'M A BELIEVER

S
he got saved.

"Saved" in the Pentecostal or holiness church, refers to when someone accepts and has faith in Jesus Christ as their Savior, believes that he died on the cross for their sins, and makes a confession of repentance for their sins, to inherit eternal life. Being a believer of the gospel and getting saved is essentially the same thing. There are outward changes in your daily living based on the confession you make with your mouth.

This is what Barbara did.

After she made that confession, she started going to church on Sundays and during the week for bible study. She surrendered her heart, mind, and body to the will of God. She stopped hanging out, smoking, and getting high. She even led the praise service at church.

Barbara could sing, y'all!

The only problem was that many of her friends, especially one particularly close friend, did not want her to be free of the tight grip drugs and alcohol had on her life. They would call the house and ask her to go out on the weekends and Barbara would respond by saying that she goes to church and does not do those things anymore. They were persistent.

Before long, their persistence had paid off. She returned to her old ways. This time the enemy returned to her with a vengeance. Barbara had yielded. All it takes is one time for someone to relapse and fall into the pitfalls of addiction. Years later, Barbara told her Mom how she wished she had never gone back and that she felt like she had done too much for the Lord to hear her prayers. Have you ever been there? A cycle of bad choices, repentance, and then more bad choices? Then you feel guilty about the bad choices you made which likely causes you to indulge in more bad choices.

I am a believer that there is good news! The good news is that God can, will, and wants to deliver us from our poor choices!

He desires so much that we prosper and be in good health, even as our soul prospers. (III John 1:2) That health includes mental health, physical health, and spiritual health. You do not have to condemn yourself over past indulgences, just bring your past to God so he can make you healthy. If you are breathing, it is never too late to get a do over. God has plans and a future for you. Have hopeI am a believer!

You may encounter many defeats, but you must not be defeated. In fact, it may be necessary to encounter the defeats, so you can know who you are, what you can rise from, how you can still come out of it.

~**Maya Angelou**

PRAYER

Lord, I confess my faults before you. I know that you are a faithful and just God who forgives me and cleanses me from all unrighteousness. I believe that Jesus died on the cross for my sins. I accept the sacrifice you made so that I can live eternally. Change my mind. Dwell in my heart. Be Lord of my life.

In Jesus' name, AMEN.

I John 1:9 (AMP)

If we [freely] admit that we have sinned and confess our sins, He is faithful and just [true to His own nature and promises], and will forgive our sins and cleanse us continually from all unrighteousness [our wrongdoing, everything not in conformity with His will and purpose].

SHOOTING GALLERIES

T
he story goes that my mom would go missing at times. No one would hear from or see her, and my grandmother would start asking around. By asking around, I mean she would go to multiple shooting galleries in pursuit of her daughter. If you do not know, a shooting gallery is a not-so-clean building, normally abandoned and dilapidated, where people would pay a few dollars to get off the street and shoot up drugs.

There were lots of people in the different rooms of the dwelling. My grandmother would demand to be let in and threatened to call the cops if they did not.

She would call out, "Barbara!" going from room to room and gallery to gallery until she found her daughter. She would drag her out of there, with full resistance from my mom. My grandmother would take her home, clean her up, and feed her. My mom could stay as long as she wanted, normally lasting no more than a couple of weeks, as the drugs would call out to her and she would succumb.

This sequence of events is much like what some of us go through as Christians. We have a loving father who comes to our aid and rescues us from the dark things we have run to, cleans us up, and gives us hope, and a future.

Not everyone stays away from the dark things, but our Father allows us to try it again and again and cheers us on, wanting us to get it right. Jeremiah 29:11

PRAYER

Thank you, Lord for being right there to free us from our own shooting gallery muck and mire. Thank you for giving us hope in our desperate situations. Thank you, God for being our redeemer and way maker. Give us strength to not return to things we know cause us harm and destruction, whether it be things or people. Thank you for your son paving the way for our victory!

In your name, AMEN

I Corinthians 10:13 (TLB)

But remember this—the wrong desires that come into your life are not anything new and different. Many others have faced the same problems before you. And no temptation is irresistible. You can trust God to keep the temptation from becoming so strong that you cannot stand up against it, for he has promised this and will do what he says.

He will show you how to escape temptation's power so that you can bear up patiently against it.

-God never promised a life of ease, but He did promise a life of victory!
– Paul Daugherty

THE UN-PASTOR

There was a man who my mom became acquainted with and we will call him Dave.

He claimed to be a pastor, but I am told that the church was a front and he ran a whore house. He was pushing drugs in the back of his building. I hate to call it a church because it really was just the opposite. He was a fake pastor, an un-pastor, who kept up his ruse by having ushers greet you at the front door. A pastor is someone who leads and shepherds a Christian congregation. I remember my mom and I getting a ride from him one time. He had a long, old white four door sedan. It reminded me of Boss Hog's vehicle, from the Dukes of Hazard, without the drop top. I felt creepy sitting in the back seat and did not know why. We went to his building during the week. No service was going on and I wondered why we were there.

We did not stay long. I now believe she was getting something to cope. He fed my mom's addiction with his supply. My grandmother was certain Dave was bringing my mom drugs to self-medicate in the hospital when she had gotten sick. The doctors told her that she still had drugs in her system, and someone must be bringing it in. Maybe my mom told Dave that she needed more pain relief than the hospital was giving. If your body is chemically dependent on a substance, you depend on it mentally and physically. You become unable to stop using it without clinical intervention even though you know it has a negative effect on your body.

My grandmother stopped visitors from coming in without her prior approval. Dave was sought out for the illegal remedy that he was bringing. I am reminded of the woman with the issue of blood in Matthew 9. She went for a long time seeking the healing that a man might provide. She wasted time and money, hoping to be made whole. When she got close to Jesus, she was healed. My mom thought she had gone too far and stayed too long to get close to Jesus, the one who heals.

PRAYER

Lord, help us to understand there is absolutely no infirmity that you do not want us healed from. All we must do is come to you instead of depending solely on the pastor, family, or friends. Thank you for giving us the same path to you as they have.

Scripture tells us in *Hebrews 4:16* (AMP) that we can:

"... *fearlessly and confidently and boldly draw near to the throne of grace (the throne of God's unmerited favor to us sinners), that we may receive mercy [for our failures] and find grace to help in good time for every need [appropriate help and well-timed help, coming just when we need it]."*

Thank you for giving us access to you at always. In Jesus' name. AMEN

There is Hope

Shawna Nicole, (Written 1995)

I know you have sorrow But lift your head up

'Cause God knows the problem.

I know you're feeling down But don't give up

'Cause God will always solve them.

He's always kept his promises He said he will never fail.

If you believe and trust in His word Through him you will prevail.

AS A SISTER

Many sisters give advice about boys and men to each other. They may argue over clothes and makeup.

A brother and sister may fuss about who gets to watch what show on television.

Well, I think it was a totally different story when it came to my mom.

This next set of passages reviews memories that have been told from the perspective of her siblings. She had one older brother, one younger brother, and one younger sister.

OLDER BROTHER

H e was the oldest, but he always said that she was his big sister. She was his buddy.

He was the firstborn, and they were less than two years apart. He was calmer and more collected, and she felt she always had to look out for him. She hovered around him. She was "that" rooster in the hen house. Early on, she would try to hook him up with her friends. One time a girl liked him, and he did not realize it. The girl started to pester him, and even threatened to beat him up after school. He recalls that his sister, Barbara got wind of it and found out the place that the girl was planning to fight him. She met the girl there and said "Don't fight my brother. Fight me!" She then 'wolfed her down' and the girl left, totally humiliated.

My mom had a big heart. She would give you the shirt off her back and was always trying to look out for others in any way that she could. This included making sure those who were close to her were taken care of. One example of my mom's big heart was when it was time for her brother to go to high school. He told my mom that he was not planning on going to Westside High School, which was the district school. The school had a frequent police presence many years ago. It was rough and tough, and he felt that was not going to be a good environment for him. Although he was her big brother, feeling like she needed to protect him, my mother said, "If anybody tries to mess with you, you just let me know." Although he ultimately chose to attend a magnet arts high school in Newark because he wanted to sharpen his talent as an artist, the statement by my mom made him feel he was never alone.

PRAYER

Lord, in everyone's life, there is both good and bad. No person is perfect and without some weakness. Even if we are a Christian, there are some areas we fall short and can be refined in. Sometimes we can overlook the good that is inside of someone because it is more popular to focus on the character flaws. Help us to look for the good in others and to promote and publicize those strengths rather than tear people down with our thoughts, words, and actions. Help us to see that we are all works in progress. Genesis 1:27 tells us "So God created man in his own image..." Because of this truth, we know that we must value and respect each person, flaws, and all. AMEN

HOW BARBARA MET JAMES

A ccording to what I hear, James was friends with Barbara's oldest brother. They were "partners" as they called it back in the 1960s and 70s. James was tall, lean, and handsome. He was at the house regularly. In fact, it was not unusual to walk in the door and see him lying on the couch, making a sandwich, or watching TV.

He was like another child to my grandmother because he was there so much. Before her mom knew it, James started "messing around" with Barbara. They were an inseparable couple. Soon after, a little baby bump appeared. It was a baby boy, and he was named James, after his father. After the birth of their first child, they were on again and off again for many months. Eventually, they got married and had another child, a daughter they named Shawna. After a while, James was no longer in the picture. They had gone their separate ways. Perhaps they were each battling their own set of issues, and it did not leave much room for them to grow together.

PRAYER

Lord, I thank you that I got to know the backstory to how my Mom met my Dad because I do not recall them together as I was growing up. It was good to know that they had at least some happy moments together and were childhood sweethearts. If for no other reason, they came together to produce two awesome kids, one of which is me.

Thank God from their production, I was able to reproduce and have 3 sons who will one day have their own children. I am convinced that even when we do not understand all the details, God has a purpose and a plan for our lives! I am blessed to know this truth! AMEN

And we know that all things work together for good to them that love the Lord, to them who are the called according to his purpose.

Romans 8:28

(Picture of James and Barbara)

CAUGHT

Have you ever been caught doing something wrong? Something you were so ashamed of you wished you could have crawled through the floor when you were found out? From what her sister remembers, I would say this was one of those times for my mom.

My mom could not have been more than 14 years old. One day, as a little girl, her sister remembers hearing my mom being told that she was going to get her behind beat. She was not wearing any clothes, and there was a man in the room. Her sister was not sure exactly how old he was, but she knew he looked older than my mom.

"I want you just like he had you." Those words rang out invariably and authoritatively from their mom.

There was a sense of heaviness in the house as things unfolded. Although her sister says the rest of the story is a blur, that moment will forever be etched in her mind. She was certain her sister was not planning to be found in that moment.

PRAYER

Lord, sometimes our guilt can cause us to wear a cloak of shame for others to see. We have all done things in our lives that we are not proud of. Help us to know that we can come to you with repentant hearts and ask earnestly for forgiveness. Thank God for faith to know that you hear us and will cleanse us from impure things. We thank you that we can throw away that cloak and walk free from guilt and shame, clothed in freedom and dignity. Thank God there is no shame in you!

In Jesus' name. AMEN

Romans 8:1-2 (NIV)

Therefore, there is now no condemnation for those who are in Christ Jesus, because through Christ Jesus the law of the Spirit who gives life has set you free from the law of sin and death.

I'M LEAVING

B y now, I think you have concluded that my mom did not 'play the radio' as the old folks say. The meaning of that is that my mom did not put up with foolishness.

The story goes that mom was pregnant with me in Florida, and my dad was there also. My brother had been born in May of the previous year. My mother thought my dad was cheating on her with someone she knew. I do not know if they physically fought or just had a verbal confrontation, but I do know that my mother left my dad in Florida and moved back to New Jersey when I was only seven days old. We are not talking weeks or years, seven DAYS old! She was done with him. I am not sure if he cheated or not, but they did not get back together. That was the end of their relationship.

I remember my father telling my grandmother when I was 13 years old that he always loved my mom, and she just would not take him back.

Perhaps my mom was too young to commit to a relationship. Maybe she despised the thought of him cheating and could not reason with herself to go back and try it again. Possibly she hated him for the way she felt and for even having to consider that he was cheating on her. Who knows?

PRAYER

Lord, help us to realize that people will let us down. Sometimes the hurt may be unintentional, but that does not make it hurt any less. Teach us to delight in the fact that you are faithful, and you will not leave us. Let us put our confidence in that truth. AMEN

Hebrews 13:5 (TLB)

"…be satisfied with what you have. For God has said, I will never, never fail you nor forsake you."

THE ASSAULT

Have you ever experienced something but was too young to remember many of the details? You are reminded of something intangible only by a pleasant or familiar smell? Something bad happened when I was around a year old, but all I could remember was the smell of cooked potatoes with onions and peppers, topped with ketchup. As weird as it sounds, I could also recall the smell of a wooden, two-pronged miniature fork. I later learned that these were some of the ingredients of something called a Jimmy Buffs sandwich that is packed into a half pita with a sausage or hot dog. This was what my brother and I were eating when there was a knock on the door.

I am told that a man tried to force his way in to our apartment. My mom was struggling to get the chain lock fastened but could not manage to secure it. I am not sure what it was all about, but I remember having a feeling of fear. One thing led to another, so I am told, and Mom began stabbing him. She stabbed him so many times, that he ended up in a wheelchair. She somehow escaped major physical harm. My mom went to jail for this.

This traumatic experience most certainly stuck with us. I cannot verify this, but I am convinced that Mom regretted her actions.

What I had seen of her was loving, witty, and jovial with streaks of firmness and sass. I cannot begin to imagine her thoughts following this event, especially being left to her own conscience in a small cell to process it all.

This was not the only time she was in jail. I remember being told she had gone a few times, but I do not know why she served time.

When we were older, my mom showed my brother and I the tattoos of our nicknames she got in jail. They were not the fancy tattoos you see adorning people's arms these days. She had the words "Pookie" and "Sha-Sha." I think "love" was there as well.

I felt proud that my mom had our names permanently on her body. Although they were not sophisticated, it showed that she was thinking of us and that we were always present no matter where she was.

As I got older, I was sensitive to how my mom must have felt in jail. Jail and prison ministry are very important parts of ministry to God.

People behind bars are often forgotten, mistreated, and written off. They need encouragement, prayers, and uplifting in their spirit. I pray there were people who took the time to visit and minister to my mom while she was in jail.

Nahum 1:7 (MSG)

God is good, a hiding place in tough times. He recognizes and welcomes anyone looking for help, no matter how desperate the trouble.

PRAYER

Lord, thank you that there are vivid stories of my mother's life to share. You are sovereign and awesome! Life is what it is today because you chose the very details of my life and have woven them together so intricately to create this beautiful tapestry called, "My Life."

I am grateful. AMEN

Hebrews 13:3 (TLB)

Don't forget about those in jail. Suffer with them as though you were there yourself. Share the sorrow of those being mistreated, for you know what they are going through.

THE ALMOST FATAL DRINK

My mother had some substance dependency. She abused alcohol and drugs while she was pregnant with me. God was in the womb providing protection from the harmful substances.

Psalm 139:13 (NIV)

For you created my inmost being; you knit me together in my mother's womb.

This seemed to affect my verbal development, making me unusually quiet. I was basically mute until I passed the age of one and my family did not think I would be able to speak.

They were shocked when one day, without any prompting, I began to talk, and not just talk – I would go on and on. I guess I was saving all my words up for just the right moment.

Then when I was 16 months old, something awful happened. My mom called my grandmother and told her that I had gotten someone's cup and drank a strong alcoholic beverage. It was so much that they had to rush me to the hospital. I may have passed out or been unresponsive. I remained in the hospital for two weeks after they pumped my stomach of its contents. They did not know if I would make it because I was very sick.

The incident was reported to the Division of Youth and Family Services (DYFS), and they told my mother that my brother and I could no longer live with her. My grandmother was not about to let us go into foster care and she took custody of us. Because she worked the second shift, it was a struggle to find someone to continue to agree to watch us until early morning.

With that in mind, my grandmother made the tough decision to send us to Florida to live with her mother Gladys, and oldest sister, Estelle. Their schedule allowed us to have adequate around-the-clock care. My brother and I got teased on several occasions when we lived with our great-aunt and great grandma. We endured cruel words like "your mother threw you away" and "your mom left you on the doorstep of your aunt." These words pierced my very soul. Although my heart told me my mom loved us, my young thoughts frequently challenged the love I felt was missing. I mean, where was she, and why didn't we see her? What was she doing? Why wasn't she here? Was she alive?

Many years passed before I knew the story behind my brother and I moving to Florida. I would hate for people to ask me how I ended up in Florida. It was a lengthy story to tell.

I know that I could not die! I had a purpose that God had already predestined. I know, however, that this event helped shape who I am today. The people I met, the places I have gone, every experience I had was all orchestrated by God himself. Every detail of my life God allowed, including that almost fatal drink.

PRAYER

Lord, we thank you for keeping us in times of adversity. We have overcome many challenges in life, all because of your grace. Even when unpleasant things happen, you place hedges of protection around us. We are thankful. AMEN

Jeremiah 1:5 (TLB)

"I knew you before you were formed within your mother's womb; before you were born I sanctified you and appointed you as my spokesman to the world."

Through Your Eyes

Shawna Nicole, 1995

Through your eyes, I see the lies

I recognize the many things that are in disguise.

With these peepers I see the hurt, the pain Of wanting a rainbow

but only getting rain.

Your eyes see wrong and right They see all that is true.

They know exactly what the future holds Even if it is not in plain

view.

God knows things would have been different It comes as no

surprise.

If I had only seen the world through your eyes.

AS A MOTHER

When I think of a mother, I think of someone who is nurturing, caring, and giving. Certainly, I believe it to be someone present in the home. By now, you know that is not how we grew up.

Although I did have a loving aunt, grandmother, and great grandmother who all had huge roles in raising me, my mother was not there regularly. In fact, she died when I was just 13 years old, and my brother was a month and a half shy of his 15th birthday.

We did not see that day coming. As a child, who believes that their mother will not be there to see them reach milestones like graduating high school, getting their first job, going off to college, getting married, or having children?

I have spent a great deal of time throughout my life wondering what she would think, do, or say in this situation or imagining the look on her face if she were there to see this or that thing happen.

I cling tightly to the memories of other's accounts, as well as the ones I have made together with the one who birthed me into this world. Do not get me wrong, the people who sacrificed their time and money and spent hours in

41

prayer and intercession on my behalf are not forgotten, nor were their hours wasted, but I am sure you can understand there is just a different kind of bond that happens between a mother and her child. This occurs no matter how many imperfections mother or child has.

Even if I were given up for adoption, I still believe that there would be a bond. I do not believe someone can carry you so close to them for such a long span of time and have absolutely no connection with that person. You are physically connected and experience many of the same things as your mother while she is carrying you.

As a mother myself, I know you carry the child through the period of conception to birth and then carry them emotionally throughout their lives.

These next stories are a recount of times my brother and I had with our mother.

TAUGHT TO FIGHT

H e was getting beat up. Every day, he would come running home because a boy was chasing him. This was the last day! My mom had come to town for a visit and she was not having any of it. She said, "If you come running home one more time, you are mine. If you lose, I'm going to beat you up!"

What motivating words! My brother, like me, had heard the stories of how strong my mom was and the intensity of her punch.

Our mom took my brother in the backyard and trained him. She showed him how and where to land a punch and how to block any incoming blows. She loved to watch boxing and she had skills.

Even though she taught my brother how to box and how to fight, I, the baby girl, was not a big fan of fighting. I was there watching from the porch, as nervous as can be. At the very thought of it, my heart raced so fast and beat so hard it felt like it would pop right out of my chest.

But my brother, on the other hand, seemed to enjoy it too much. After the lesson, he was always up for a good fight and could be seen fighting at school or in the neighborhood. From then on, I cannot recall a time my brother lost a fight. Even if he did, my mom surely never knew about it. Fighting is something my brother certainly had in common with my mom.

While I cannot say that my mom taught me to fight physically, she had a message behind her teaching. I believe she always wanted us to win. No matter what the battle or obstacle, we were taught to overcome the challenge.

My mom wanted to make sure we knew we were victorious in our lives and not victims. She did not want my brother to be defeated as a guy. She knew he would one day grow up to be a man.

She fought and won for those she loved, just as Jesus has already won the fight for us.

PRAYER

May we continue to fight the right kind of fight spiritually, in the power of Jesus and not in our own strength.

"But thanks be to God, which giveth us the victory through our Lord Jesus Christ."

1 Corinthians 15:57

THE FISHING TRIP

My mom, brother, and I woke up early one Saturday morning, as any good fisherman knows to do. We had our bait and tackle box filled with all the needed items to catch some unsuspecting fish.

We had a cooler/bucket to transport the catchings of the day.

Drinks were tossed into the cooler. She had her beer and we had our soda.

Our mom was going to show us how to fish, and we were excited! We had our bamboo poles in hand as we headed for the bridge. We arrived, picked out the perfect spot, and the teaching commenced. My brother and I had grown more excited by the minute as we listened intently to the instructions. Mom cast her line, got a big bite, and proceeded to show us how to reel in the fish. Little did we know, it was a baby shark, and instead of reeling it in, it pulled her over the pier into the water. She fell over, cigarette in mouth and pole in hand. I can recall a few choice expletives as she began her descent. I am pretty sure she did not know how to swim. She was flailing her arms in the water and bobbing up and down trying to get us to call for help.

My brother and I were both scared and stunned. There was a paralyzing feeling that came over me. We were screaming and yelling for help! A man appeared from, I believe, the fish market, and this is where my recollection grows dim. I just remember the man, somehow getting our mother out of the water and back to safety and to us.

When she came out, she was cut up from the rocks and the oyster beds. She obviously was soaking wet and cold from the early morning water.

The very short-lived training was officially over. We gathered our belongings for the return journey. The trek back home was mostly somber and quiet, but we were all very thankful that mom was still with us. It seemed to be the longest walk I had ever taken.

For me to say that this was a traumatizing experience is an understatement. I just knew deep in my heart that our mom was gone. I immediately began trying to figure out how I was going to cross the busy street and get safely back home without my mom. How was I going to explain to our family and friends what happened? My mind was running rampant. I was only about six or seven years old and had always had a vivid imagination. This time it got the best of me. I went fishing a time or two after this incident, but I could not help but be reminded of that day when I first flung my line into the water. The memory is still a very vivid one.

PRAYER

God, I thank you for not letting my mom die during our fishing trip. You were right there to preserve and keep her in that time. You are all-knowing and all-powerful. Just like you protected her, you are no respecter of person and can keep us as well.

Psalm 121:7 (AMP)

The Lord will protect you from all evil; He will keep your life.

AMBUSHED

W̲e were living in a haven. We had our routines down and our traditions established. From doing daily chores and watching Worldwide Wrestling Federation on Friday nights, to playing in the backyard and going on adventures in the "woods" surrounding our house.

Without warning, we were thrust into an uncomfortable series of events. We will call him Darryl. He was the one at the time. The one who had connections to get my mother the stuff she craved. It was obvious. He was not clean shaven or even handsome. He looked a little frightening to me. Darryl wore a khaki-colored trench coat and had dark, beady eyes that seemed to peer right through you. I do not recall his voice or remember anything pleasant about him. No kind words, just an evil presence. He would ride over on his bicycle to see my mom while she was in St. Augustine visiting us.

Darryl seemed very out of place. During that time, two incidents happened. In retrospect, my mom may have owed him money for the "stuff" he was providing. We came home one day to find my mother had been severely beaten. Her face was swollen, lips busted, and her eye was purple. We were shocked! Until then, we had only heard of how tough my mother was and how she liked to fight. I would surmise that she was embarrassed for us to see her like that.

Days later, we came home to yet another shock. Our house had been broken into. The front door was kicked in. TVs were gone, bikes missing, belongings damaged. We were all so upset and worried. My great-grandmother told her that her house had never been broken into as long as she had lived there and that it was time for my mom to leave.

My brother and I were devastated. We never saw Darryl again, but it did not stop me from expecting him to return to our house.

PRAYER

Lord it is so comforting to know we have a loving father to trust.
Thank you for reminding me to put my confidence and trust in
you oh God and to not fear. AMEN

Joshua 1:9 (TLB)

*Yes, be bold and strong! Banish fear and doubt! For remember, the Lord
your God is with you wherever you go.*

Psalm 56:3-4 (NIV)

*When I am afraid, I put my trust in you. In God, whose word I praise—
in God I trust and am not afraid. What can mere mortals do to me?*

DOING MY HAIR

When I was about nine years old, my brother and I went to New Jersey to visit our grandmother for the summer. When there, we would visit our mom's house here and there.

This time we visited, she did my hair in these little ponytails with the blue and red round ponytail holders and matching barrettes that coordinated with my outfit. I was cute, and I knew it.

Right after she finished, I asked if I could go outside and play. She agreed.

I remember her getting angry about me being outside playing with the boys. They were chasing me and giving me lots of attention. Obviously, they thought I was cute, too. I could hear the disdain in her voice as she called down to me from the 2nd floor window, "Sha'-Sha', come here!" (That was, and still is, my nickname.) Parents have a way of calling your name that lets you know they are not happy.

So, I marched upstairs, disappointed that my playtime had been interrupted. I was greeted by, "Don't let them boys touch you; boys are bad! As a matter of fact, do not go back downstairs while all those boys are outside."

I was so hurt. There were no girls on the entire block, it seemed, so I was stuck in the house.

My mom was vigilant and very protective.

Possibly, she had witnessed someone else experience some unfortunate events. In her mind, she very well could have been protecting me from a repeat of her own experiences. As I grew older, I was able to better relate to the words she spoke back then. There were several boys who challenged me sexually. Some were more forceful and persistent, and others were less aggressive but still very forward. God protected me in each of those times.

PRAYER

Lord, I thank you for my mom's discernment and protection in this instance. Although I was not living with her, she clearly cared about me and wanted what was best for me. Looking back, I know she was trying to shield me from potential poor juvenile choices. We thank God that even as my mom was protecting me from potential snares, our heavenly father provides the same protection for us from the wiles of the enemy.

That's right—he rescues you from hidden traps, shields you from deadly hazards. His huge, outstretched arms protect you—under them you're perfectly safe; his arms fend off all harm.

Psalm 91:3-4 (MSG)

TIME WITH MR. PETE

M r. Pete was an older man. He was at least 20 years older than my mom. You could tell he loved my mother, and from what I could tell she was fond of him too.

Mr. Pete had two adult daughters who lived on the 1st floor of his three-story house, a teenage son, and a son around my age. They all appeared to love my mother as well. I enjoyed going over to his house because it was big and there were kids outside to play with. I remember that I would always get spoiled when I went. Mr. Pete would put food on the grill for us to eat, or we would go to a place called Bowcraft in Scotch Plains.

Bowcraft was like a miniature Six Flags Great Adventures. It had an arcade, putt-putt golf, and amusement rides. It appeared very expensive to me, but Mr. Pete did not seem to mind. Mr. Pete's kids called my mom Ms. Barb. That was fine with me. It had a nice ring to it. The thing I did not like was that she lived there with them and not us. I remember that I always wanted to sleep over at Mr. Pete's house just so I could pretend that I lived with my mother, even for just one night. That never happened.

I was ok with Mr. Pete's kids, but I was terribly jealous that they seemed to be her children more than I was. She fixed their food, helped them with their homework, talked to them about important school matters, and did their laundry–all the stuff moms do for their own kids. It seemed to me, even as a kid that though moms can help other kids, their own children should come first. After all, she carried us in her belly, we kicked her while we lived inside of her for all those months. The bonds between mothers and their own children should have been unbreakable. The more I thought about it, the more resentment grew inside of me.

I knew, as I got older, I had to take the time to process my feelings of resentment and release them to the Lord so I could heal.

Since I could not do much about the fact that I did not live with my mom, I vowed to myself at a very early age that things would be different when I had children.

Like most mothers, I cannot say that I am perfect, but I did and am doing my best.

PRAYER

Thank you Lord for the ability to look at things that happened in our past as learning opportunities. You helped me to identify sources of anger, jealousy, and resentment so that I could release those feelings and live a healthy and prosperous life. I can detect when those feelings try to arise again and address them before they take root in my heart. Thank you God for clarity. I thank you that you allowed me to see my jealous ways and release those feelings to you so that I can live a healthy and prosperous life.

In Jesus' name. AMEN

Proverbs 14:30 (NIV)

A heart at peace gives life to the body, but envy rots the bones.

Psalm 51:10 (TLB)

Create in me a new, clean heart, O God, filled with clean thoughts and right desires.

WHO WAS SHAVON?

O ne day, when I was about 12 and visiting with my mom, we were walking down Springfield Avenue when she told me she needed to do something. She told me to wait and that she would be right back as she hurried across the street. My mom did not tell me where she was going and gave no explanation when she returned. It seemed she was gone forever but it was no longer than 30 minutes. She told a young lady to watch me while she was gone. We will call her Shavon, and she looked to be about 18 or 19 years old. Shavon was a tall, slender girl with short hair and baggy jeans, a camisole top with an open longsleeved plaid shirt. She asked my age and tried to make small talk. I was curious how she knew my mom because I had never seen or heard of her before. I never got a straight answer as to how they met.

Shavon said, "you have a good mom, I wish I had a mom like her. Ms. Barbara looks out for me and makes sure I'm ok." More questions erupted from my mouth, but no explanations followed. She told me to make sure I stayed in school and got good grades so I would not have to be like her. I cannot remember every detail of the conversation we had, but I recall feeling sorry for Shavon because she had been out on her own since the age of 15. How and what did she eat? Where was her family and where did she live? Did she have a job? In a city like Newark, I do not think it was her choice to be out there.

It appeared quite rough and scary to me as a 12-year-old. I remember often going to the corner store down the street from where we lived and having to walk past drunk men and seemingly addicts.

Many times, they would make comments about how pretty I was. I was so afraid I decided to try to look as mean and tough as I could so they would not bother me. I guess it worked because they never made a move. I had not thought about Shavon for many, many years. Then one day unexpectedly and uncontrollably, I began to weep for Shavon. I did not have her phone number, last name, or any way to contact her. I was over a thousand miles from Newark. I was not sure she was still alive or that she even remembered that day we met. Her memory was so strong in that moment that I had to release the deep sorrow I had felt for the way she lived.

Sometimes the way other people experience life can have a major impact on the way we choose to live our life. I had determined certain criteria for my life before I became an adult. I knew that I would not drink or smoke, not because I was better than anyone else, but because I saw the effects of what it did to the people I loved so dearly. I decided that I would try my best and be successful, whatever that looked like, not because I was more worthy than others, but rather I did not want to live in the streets or in uncertainty like Shavon.

I do not know who Shavon really was. I do know that there are many Shavons out there. Good people but may have made some bad decisions. My heart goes out to them.

This encounter changed my life. Thank you Shavon for giving me something to pray for.

PRAYER & DECLARATION

Lord, I pray for all the "Shavons" in this world. There are so many women who feel hopeless for themselves and have all the hope for others. Sometimes we can be afraid to hope because we feel that we have gone through so much. She was hopeful for me but had lost all hope for herself at such a young age. I pray that you send more "Shavons" my way and that I can be a beacon of light and hope for.

Make this declaration: It runs in my family until it ran into me! I am the one to break the cycle.

Generational curses stop with me. No more.

I have hope!

I have peace like a mighty river. I have got the victory!

Psalm 25:5 (TLB)

Lead me; teach me; for you are the God who gives me salvation. I have no hope except in you.

Psalm 46:5 (NIV)

God is within her, she will not fall; God will help her at break of day.

ABSENCE MAKES THE HEART GROW FONDER?

A ll I know is that when I saw my mom, I do not remember my dad anywhere around. I resented the fact that he decided to move on. How could he? How could he be with another lady after he said "I do" to my mom? Then, he had the nerve to give this other lady two children and act as if we we are not his firstborn kids? He did not reach out to us regularly to find out if we needed anything. Our absence did not make his heart grow fonder. I can count on both hands the times I recall seeing my dad as a child.

Once, he picked my brother and I up from my grandma's house and took us to meet our sisters who were living a few blocks away. He seemed so excited and was doting on us! I was nine and my brother had just turned eleven. I remember that we walked down the street and stopped at the corner store. My dad bought me brother and I each a bag of Big Bols. Big Bols is a pink candy-covered gum. I had never had one before and was excited that my dad had bought us anything at all. I think he spent $2.00 total on the both of us, but it did not matter at the time. To this day, I get excited at the sight of Big Bols.

That is the last time that I recall him ever spending any money on us. I guess he had another family who demanded his money, time, and attention. After all, he was living with them. I was again disappointed by the fact that other children seemed to be in the position that me brother and I rightfully deserved. Although, through my father's second union we gained two younger sisters who we came to know and love, it was as if we were erased from his memory.

That is how I felt. I felt gypped. For years, I carried around anger and resentment that my mom and dad were not together. At some point, I made a conscious decision to let go of all that bitterness because it did not benefit me in any way. I asked God for a release from the resentment so I could move on to a place of freedom.

If you are having these feelings towards someone, I encourage you to let it go. ALL of it.

Hebrews 12:15 (MSG)

Keep a sharp eye out for weeds of bitter discontent. A thistle or two gone to seed can ruin a whole garden in no time.

63

PRAYER

Help us Lord to not hold grudges about things that happened so many years ago and were not done with ill intentions. We cannot change the things that were done. Thank you for giving us the revelation that we can not keep putting people in a space they do not have the capacity to fill. Help us to forgive and move on from the past. Help us to forgive and move on from the past.

…But this one thing I do, forgetting those things which are behind, and reaching forth unto those things which are before, I press toward the mark for the prize of the high calling of God in Christ Jesus.

Philippians 3:13

NEW DIET

I recall a time I was visiting my mother, and she was baking French fries. Who does that? I immediately questioned the rationale behind it. I was about twelve years old. I said, "Mommy, why are you putting the French fries in the oven?" I received a stern scowl of disapproval and an entire lecture about how fried French fries were not good for you and baked fries were much healthier. I happened to love fried French fries a lot. I loved watching them fry up into golden perfection, nicely firm and crisp. I was not at all excited to eat the somewhat lackluster fries that were pulled from the oven. They looked pale in comparison to the ones I enjoyed eating, pun intended. Once I tasted them, I decided they were not that bad after all. I still today mostly eat them baked at home.

My mom's diet had drastically changed. It had to. She would pull the skin from the chicken and bake it. In fact, she had cut out all fried foods and would eat as healthy as her money and taste buds would allow. Later, I found out that the doctors advised her to eat this way.

Shawna Nicole

PRAYER

Thank you, God that my mom had the inclination to take the suggestion of the doctors and modify her diet. Making healthy changes for the better are not always easy to do. Whether it be diet or other poor habits, God give us the strength and commitment to do the thing.

Proverbs 16:3 (NIV)

Commit to the LORD whatever you do, and he will establish your plans.

THAT CALL

I remember getting a phone call from my mother a couple of months before she died. That memory will forever be etched in stone in my mind. It was a very bitter and unexpected experience. I never saw the blow coming when I answered the phone.

I answered, "Hey Mommy," because we had caller id. That had become popular back in those days, so I fully expected her voice on the other end when I noticed the number. She was never one for beating around the bush. So, there were no drawn out formalities or long to dos. She immediately asked me if I was afraid of her? I grew numb at the question. My lips would not part. She said, "Sha-Sha, ANSWER ME! Are you afraid of me?" I reluctantly and somberly said, "Yes ma'am."

She began to weep, and it ripped me in two. She managed to get out the words, "Why? Why are you afraid of me?" She had a way of demanding an answer, and she fully deserved one.

She was my mother, after all. I stuttered and scrambled for the words to put her mind at ease. There were none. I could only state the truth. The truth is that HIV/AIDS was a new and uncertain disease, and doctors were still in the early stages of finding out how it is transmitted, and how to avoid contracting it from someone else. Our family, particularly my grandmother and I, were both concerned and careful about how we interacted with my mom to avoid accidental contraction. We were so careful in fact, that it raised red flags to my mother to the point she had to ask questions.

She was still waiting for an answer, the answer I lamented over. I finally uttered the words, "I don't want to get sick like you!" I said it. I was completely ashamed of the fact that I had to say it. I was ashamed that it was even an issue. I was ashamed because I was afraid of my own mother.

How did she get to this point? Why do we have to travel down this road? Is this really the point of no return? Can we please, please turn back the hands of time to where I do not have to witness the change in her hair texture, the weight loss, frequent hospitalizations, and the harsh dietary restrictions?

This was a tough road to travel down. Looking back, this conversation with my mom, albeit very emotion-filled, will always be near and dear to me. I am glad I was able to release those words.

PRAYER

Lord, I am young, and I am scared. My grandmother told me that my mom is dying if the Lord does not work a miracle. My mom is giving my grandmother legal custody of me so it can be easier to go to the doctor and dentist. Well Lord, I am asking you to work a miracle because I still want my mom around.

I know we do not live together, but I know that she wants to see me more. I know she wants to see me graduate from 13th Avenue and move on to high school. I believe you can do it Lord. I have been taught to have faith even if it is the size of a mustard seed, and it can move a mountain. Watching my mom be sick and lose weight looks like a big mountain to me. Can you move this mountain, Lord? I just want her to get better and be around a lot longer. Please Lord! In Jesus' name, AMEN.

Psalm 3:5-6 (MSG)

Trust GOD from the bottom of your heart; don't try to figure out everything on your own. Listen for GOD's voice in everything you do, everywhere you go; he's the one who will keep you on track.

THE LAST CALL

My grandmother and I were in our beds asleep. By this time, my mom had been in and out of the hospital for many months. It was very tough on my grandmother to see her child in so much pain and agony. It was tough on me not being able to go to the hospital to see her.

At around midnight, the phone rang, and my grandma starts screaming, "No, no, no!" I woke up, and I knew immediately what was going on. I do not think I cried, but I felt really, sad. I was numb and did not know what to do or say. I could not comfort her, because I was in shock.

PRAYER

Oh, my Lord! My grandmother just got the call that my mom died! No Lord! I cannot believe this! I prayed Lord. I believed Lord! Why is she gone? I am only 13 years old! My brother is not even 15 yet! How will I know how she feels about all the stuff I must go through in life? Why do I have to keep living without my mom? My grandmother has just lost her oldest daughter, and she is very, very sad. I am sad. My brother is sad. Our family is hurting. I thought you loved me God! I do not think this is right at all! I want my mother back! I do not think I want to talk to you because I am hurting badly. My head seems foggy like I am in a bad dream. I just want to see her face looking at me right now. This is too hard for me to bear. Please tell me they made a mistake and my mom is still alive. Even though we did not live together, we still had a relationship.

Help me Lord!

Jeremiah 17:14 (MSG)

God, pick up the pieces. Put me back together again. You are my praise!

(My 7th Grade class at 13th Avenue School)

A BLACK GIRL TALKS OF WEEPING

Shawna Nicole, 1994

I have wept for many days I wish that it would cease.

I want the Lord to comfort my heart and provide me inner peace.

Comfort my mortal mind and take away the pain.

Destroy the confusion in my life give me knowledge to gain-

A foothold in my life is what I am asking for.

A life filled with prosperity and only minute flaws.

Nothing less, nothing more.

CONCLUSION

A nd so, it begins. The next chapters of my life started to unfold as I came to the reality that my mother had died. I did not know exactly how to feel. I was devastated, although I outwardly kept a nonchalant air, trying to detach from my feelings. I kept on moving even though I really did not know how. I did my best to keep a straight face at school and did what I was told.

I really felt like a part of me died that day in April 1990. I was almost finished with the 7th grade. I excelled in my studies at school but not emotionally.

My face had a cloak of sadness that I wore for a long time. It was not because no one loved me. It was because I missed my mom and often thought of how things would have been if she were still alive. Not long after that, my grandmother became ill with a severe case of sinusitis. I am sure it was due to the grief of losing her child. My brother was missing his mom as well. Family members were trying their very best to cope after death had snatched my mom, but it was not easy.

PRAYER

God, I thank you that although my mother passed away, I know she would have been proud of many of the decisions I have made. My confidence has not always been the best, but I am owning more and more of who I am and where I came from. I love you Mommy, and I will never forget you and the experiences we had!

Lord, I thank you that she told me she loved me, and I was able to wholeheartedly believe it. Lord I thank you for her example. Sometimes people teach you what not to do by their example, and I totally got it.

I appreciate you, Lord, for not letting me slip into wrong ways so much that it took me out. I am not perfect by any means, but I am transforming into who you have called me to be, layer by layer. In Jesus' name. AMEN

Psalm 68:19 (AMP)

Blessed be the Lord, who bears our burden day by day, The God who is our salvation!

Romans 15:13 (AMP)

May the God of hope fill you with all joy and peace in believing [through the experience of your faith] that by the power of the Holy Spirit you will abound in hope and overflow with confidence in His promises.

FORGIVENESS

For many years, I have struggled with issues of unforgiveness. Any time someone crossed me or intentionally mistreated me, I would secretly compartmentalize my feelings towards them and it likely surfaced in our relationship. Over time, that takes up so much space mentally that it can overtake your life with negative thoughts of people overall. I realize that it does me no good and it does not hurt the other person(s) when you keep all the negative feelings inside. It is literally poison and it causes your thoughts to be suspicious of others without any justification. I had to come to a decision of whether I would continue this dangerous path. I chose to forgive.

I forgive every single person who ever hurt, mishandled, and abused my mom, both physically, sexually, and emotionally. There were countless unknown stories of my mom being subjected to things that caused her to be bitter and angry, and promoted self-medication to cope with past trauma.

I forgive those who have hurt both me and my loved ones. I understand how my mom felt when people would mistreat or mishandle her family. It makes you angry. I had begun to hold on to anger and bitterness as well for many things that were not even my anger to feel. This causes undue stress and causes you to block where God is trying to take you.

Forgiving others helps me to be free to live without resentment and frees me to love unconditionally. I am better able to accept the love and forgiveness that Jesus Christ died on the cross to give and stop beating myself up over the mistakes that I have made or will make in the future.

By forgiving, I am also resting in the fact that my God is sovereign, and He says that vengeance is his and that means I need not worry about evildoers.

Truth be told, I also had to come to forgive God! You read that right. I had to forgive God because I was angry that he took my mom, my sister and other loved ones. I was also bitter because I felt like He let me walk out some difficult things I knew he could have spared me from. I now realize that those trials only made me stronger, even when I felt I was weak and would crumble under the pressure. Forgiving God is like a closed fist being opened. For years, I would not let anyone into certain spaces of my heart, not even God. Now, I have opened my heart up to a deeper relationship with Him, one that is growing to new levels.

It was his will for me to know Him deeper.

Jeremiah 24:7 (AMP)

I will give them a heart to know Me, [understanding fully] that I am the LORD; and they will be My people, and I will be their God, for they will return to Me with their whole heart.

THE MASK

Shawna Nicole, 2002

The mask that no one wants to wear. The mask, does anybody
really care?
The mask, tell someone? – you better not dare!
With it, you have a feeling of despair Because the burden no one
wants to share. The mask, the pain it brings cannot compare The
mask, it just is not fair.
The mask, it has a phony glare.

The mask conceals true feelings inside The mask covers things
you are trying to hide.
The mask will not reveal the true you because of pride.

You have a much happier side But it frequently seems to have
died.
The mask, something everyone has tried The mask, by wearing it,
to others you have lied The mask, behind it many times have you
cried.

The mask, will you allow it to be unsealed So that the true you
might be revealed?

Or will you continue to pretend and there will be no end
To the false happiness you portray.

The poem above was written many years ago as I reminisced about the loss of my dearest family members and the deep sadness that I felt. I tried to hide behind a mask or façade that everything was ok, but losing loved ones can be very difficult, especially early in life.

Maybe you have felt this way, like you were walking around trying to keep it all together and still function while on the inside you feel so many unexplainable emotions. You feel no one has ever experienced the deep pain and loss that you have. That is a lie!

The Bible tells us that there is nothing new under the sun. Ecclesiastes 1:9

The Bible also tells us that we can cast our burdens on the Lord because he cares for us. I Peter 5:7

Today, I want you to take off your mask!

Throw it away. No more pity parties! There is too much greatness hiding behind that mask and people are desperately waiting for your greatness to manifest!

You have much MORE to offer! You CAN smile and LIVE again!

No one told us that life would be easy, but we can take assurance in the fact that God is sovereign, and he promises to be with us and never leave us!

ABOUT THE AUTHOR

Shawna currently lives in Montgomery, Alabama with her awesome husband of more than 20 years and their 3 sons. She was born in St. Augustine, Florida but has deep roots in Newark, New Jersey where she attended middle school, high school, and Rutgers University for 2 years before venturing into the Air Force.

Shawna served as the Prison Ministry Liaison for over 7 years through her local church. The ministry team would enter a Maximum-Security Women's Prison once a month sharing the good news of the gospel. This ministry was birthed from the desire to bring hope to those incarcerated who need to be introduced to and/or reminded of the grace of God even in their current circumstances. God's love reaches across any barrier!

She holds a master's degree in Vocational Rehabilitation Counseling and works for a local non-profit organization where she assists clients with learning disabilities pursue higher education.

Shawna has a love for baking and teaching. She enjoys spending time with family and friends, reading, and learning new things.

www.ingramcontent.com/pod-product-compliance
Lightning Source LLC
Chambersburg PA
CBHW060424090426
42734CB00011B/2442